Friendly Fire

"Our work focuses
on projects that
involve issues
of sustainability
and community
involvement."

—MATTHEW MCGUINNESS, THE 62

"Our motto is 'Form Honors Vision.' It identifies what our company is all about: the process of coaxing an idea into reality."

—CALEB CRYE, CRYE ASSOCIATES

"Yes, I'm a farmer."

—HUBERT MCCABE, THE 62

"...one day we just
called the army and
asked if they needed
help."

—CALEB CRYE, CRYE ASSOCIATES

"We got involved
in anti-war rallies,
for example, and
designed posters
especially for
these events."

—MATTHEW MCGUINNESS, THE 62

"I was raised a liberal in Canada. My parents are shocked and dismayed by what I do."

—ERIC FEHLBERG, CRYE ASSOCIATES

"Where Caleb sees a
flying car, I see the
Staten Island landfill.
One of the things that
we're trying to do
in The 62 is to take
our responsibility
as graphic designers
seriously."

—MATTHEW MCGUINNESS, THE 62

"...you're never going to get any progress unless you're willing to invest in a project and put your name on it and say, 'I think this is going to help people and I'm going to stand behind it.'"

—CALEB CRYE, CRYE ASSOCIATES

Fresh Dialogue Six / New Voices in Graphic Design

Friendly Fire

Princeton Architectural Press
American Institute of Graphic Arts New York Chapter
New York, 2006

Published by
Princeton Architectural Press
37 East Seventh Street
New York, New York 10003

For a free catalog of books, call 1.800.722.6657.
Visit our website at www.papress.com.

ISBN 1-56898-582-7
ISBN 978-1-56898-582-4

Editing: Nicola Bednarek
Design: Jan Haux + Deb Wood

Special thanks to: Nettie Aljian, Dorothy Ball, Janet Behning,
Becca Casbon, Penny (Yuen Pik) Chu, Russell Fernandez, Clare Jacobson, John
King, Mark Lamster, Nancy Eklund Later, Linda Lee, Katharine Myers, Lauren
Nelson, Scott Tennent, Jennifer Thompson, Paul G. Wagner, and Joseph Weston of
Princeton Architectural Press
—Kevin C. Lippert, publisher

Library of Congress Cataloging-in-Publication Data is available
from the publisher.

Contributors:
Crye Associates: Caleb Crye and Eric Fehlberg
The 62: Matthew McGuinness and Hubert McCabe

Moderator:
James Victore

Date:
10 June 2005

Location:
Fashion Institute of Technology

Contents:

How the hell can anything, let alone a dialogue, stay fresh for twenty-plus years? And yet that is exactly what the New York Chapter of the American Institute of Graphic Arts (AIGA) has done with Fresh Dialogue; it has kept the conversation going—fresh and vital. The goal of Fresh Dialogue is to present to the design community new, emerging, and important voices in design. This year, with the support of my co-chair John Fulbrook, we not only kept it fresh, but we made it current.

In a time when the United States are less "united" than "red" or "blue," we felt we could not relinquish ourselves to a pretty picture show. The participants for the 2005 event were chosen based on the traditional criteria of being young, vital, and...fresh, but in addition they both brought another element to the table—controversy. We chose two studios from the fringe, from the edges of design. In fact, the only person on stage to admit that he was actually a designer was me, the moderator. The AIGA received a certain amount of flack for putting these two groups on stage. Not only did we lose our sponsor for the event due to their worries about the content, but we also received angry late-night phone calls from "concerned" friends. We took it as an indication that the evening we were planning was truly going to be "fresh."

The 62 is a "super-amazing cultural garage," a collaborative formed of graffiti artists, political hotheads, and an organic farmer. As a group they have created beautiful and poetic works for museums, galleries, and other culturally concerned institutions. Their counterparts, Crye Associates, are self-proclaimed "industrial optimists" whose clients include the U.S. Army and the police and fire departments. Their first project with the military was the redesign of the army's camouflage pattern, which is now in the collection of the Cooper-Hewitt, National Design Museum.

What became most evident during the course of the evening was not the differences that lie between these two,

14

but the striking similarities they share: the love of making things, a passion for their work, and the belief that they are working to create better worlds. They both give a damn.

Thanks to Princeton Architectural Press we are able to recreate the evening here in these pages. It is our hope that reading this book, you feel the energy and humor but also the possibilities and opportunities we posses in design—opportunities to make change, to make comment, and to remain fresh.

Music/background
conversation

The four
panelists sit
center stage
in front of a
large projection
screen. To their
left, a podium
is set up.

Enter JAMES
VICTORE

Who We Are and What We Do

JAMES VICTORE **Good evening everybody and welcome to Fresh Dialogue. I want to start this evening by having our two studios introduce themselves. We'll begin with Crye Associates.**

CALEB CRYE I'm managing director of Crye Associates, a company I founded in 2000 with Karen Chen from Cornell and two of my fellow students at Cooper Union, Eric Fehlberg and Gregg Thompson. We do mainly engineering and industrial design; our work ranges from simple houseware products to military items. Our office is located in the Brooklyn Navy Yard.

MATTHEW MCGUINNESS The 62 is an art and design collaborative, which was founded in 2002 by Hubert McCabe, Andrei Kallaur, Morgan Sheasby, and myself. Our work focuses on projects that involve issues of sustainability and community involvement. We're also located in the Brooklyn Navy Yard.

CRYE ASSOCIATES™

Form Honors Vision

VICTORE **It's interesting that both your studios are in the Brooklyn Navy Yard environment. One is on the inside of the fence, the other on the outside. Caleb and Eric, do you want to start by talking about some of Crye Associates's work?**

CRYE Our motto is "Form Honors Vision." It identifies what our company is all about: the process of coaxing an idea into reality.

ERIC FEHLBERG One of our first projects was a new camouflage pattern that we developed for the U.S. Army as part of a new uniform design we did for them. The idea was to create a pattern that would blend in with all sorts of different environments. Currently, the army has two uniforms with different camouflage patterns for operating in the woods and in the desert. In addition, they have all this other equipment, part of which is only available in one or the other pattern. This became a problem almost fifteen years ago during the first Gulf War, when the soldiers were equipped with desert uniforms but also had to wear gear that came only in the darker camouflage pattern. As a result, they ended up not blending in anywhere. The same happened during the war in Afghanistan, which was around the time when we started working for the army. So we came up with the idea of developing just one pattern that didn't stick out too badly anywhere. The military thought it was impossible, but we wanted to at least try it. To be honest with you, we actually thought it might be impossible, too.

Our first attempt was really beautiful and subtle and looked like a painting. It didn't work at all.

CRYE It was almost too subtle.

FEHLBERG It glowed bright blue at dawn and dusk, and it looked flat, as if it was just one color. After several design iterations, we developed the final pattern, which is called MultiCam™. As you can see, it blends in better than the old patterns in both environments.

During the design process, we looked at several different sources. We did research on animals that live in these kinds of environments and examined the colors of their skin or fur. We noticed that their colors often fade from light to dark and are a kind of middle gray or brown. There're no pure greens or blacks. It's not that these animals blend in, they just don't really stand out.

VICTORE **Eric, are those PMS colors? How did you pick them?**

FEHLBERG I made little gouache swatches that we tried to match to PMS colors. But the funny thing is that they don't actually match any PMS colors. They're just these muddy, crappy colors that you can't really name or match to any system we've found.

Laughter

VICTORE **Is MultiCam™ trademarked for Crye Associates or Crye Precision?**

FEHLBERG It's overly complicated. Crye Precision is essentially the production branch of our company and Crye Associates is where the design work happens. So Crye Associates designed and patented MultiCam™, while Crye Precision licenses the right to use it.

CRYE We were really happy with MultiCam™, and it was a big success for us. The design was exhibited in the Extreme Textiles show at the Cooper-Hewitt in spring of 2004 and has also been accepted into the collection of the Museum of Modern Art. And on top of that, Supreme, Arc'teryx, and several other urban-wear companies are currently using it.

FEHLBERG The army, though, didn't feel that it was the right look for their current uniform. They've adopted another camouflage pattern, which is different from ours, for their current gear.

VICTORE **Oh, they want their own?**

FEHLBERG Yes. Sometimes that's just the way it goes.

HUBERT MCCABE The first project we worked on, in the fall of 2003, was the Fourtealizer, a fertilizer made from a nitrogen-rich condensation collected from decomposing vegetable matter called worm tea. It was a byproduct of a project we were doing in our kitchen, where we had started composting all of our kitchen scraps with red wriggler worms, the classic worm used for fishing. In October '03 the Fourtealizer and our packaging for it was part of a group show called Renewable Brooklyn at Prospect Park. The theme of the exhibition was sustainability and eco-friendly technology, art, and design. In our work for the show we used design to illustrate a different way of approaching waste, especially kitchen waste, which we all produce. For the most part, this kind of waste gets dumped into landfills, although it actually is an amazing fertilizer.

A line on the bottles tells you how much you have to dilute the liquid before you pour it on your plants. In addition, we used illustrations to talk about garbage and recycling and different waste products.

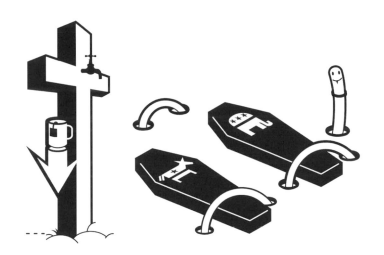

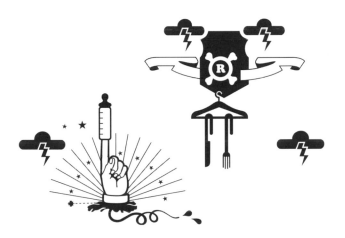

VICTORE **What are you, a farmer?**

Laughter

MCCABE Yes, I'm a farmer.

Laughter

We actually ended up trucking most of the Fourtealizer that was produced for the show up to my farm in upstate New York where we put it on my pepper plants.

CRYE The Future Force Warrior is probably the biggest project we've done so far. We started working on it about two years ago, and it's still ongoing. It takes up about 60 percent of our work. Basically, the Future Force Warrior, which was originally called the Scorpion Project, is a redesign of everything the soldier wears and carries from the ground up, except for his weapon and his helmet. Those are separate projects, although we did work on the helmet in the beginning and developed a prototype with integrated communications equipment, higher protection levels, and night vision.

Soldier equipment had never been designed as a complete system before. So, for example, a backpack guy designed the backpack, and the clothing people designed the clothes. As a result, it's just a big confabulation of gear and straps and crap. So the idea was to replace the entire pile of gear soldiers currently wear with clothing and equipment designed as a system.

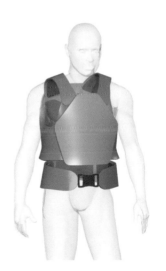

VICTORE **How did you get involved in this project? How did the army know of Crye Associates?**

CRYE When we started our company, we decided that we wanted to do military projects simply because we'd always been impressed with the design of military products. Not knowing how to go about that, one day we just called the army and asked if they needed help. We happened to call the right place, and they actually did need help. If we had called the year before or the year after, they would probably have said "Who are you? Go away." But at the time, they were in a crunch. They wanted new, fresh ideas and needed someone to design a complete new system from the ground up. We were extremely cheap compared to the General Dynamics/Lockheed-type companies they usually work with.

Laughter

So they said, "Here's what we'll do: We'll pay the big defense contractor guys to do it. But we'll also pay you a little bit, and we'll see who designs the best system." At the end of the project, they conducted a user jury with actual soldiers to decide which proposal they preferred. When the jury met, some of the soldiers actually got up and left while the big defense contractors' design was presented. They said, "We've got things to do, we don't have time for this." Our system had to be brought out to keep them interested, which was a nice compliment.

And then we raised our prices and kept working on the project.

Laughter

Designing every piece so that it fits into the overall system and everything works together was actually quite hard because soldiers work in a lot of different environments, and there are many different extreme-use cases. What is interesting is that I think we got the job partially because our proposal looked very good. None of the other firms had given the army any concepts or good ideas to begin with, whereas our proposal was full of drawings and sketches and concepts.

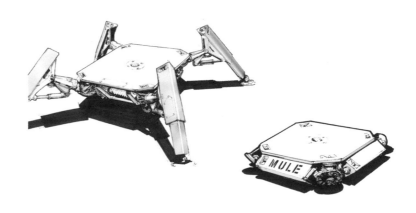

VICTORE **What did the other guys give them, just lunch?**

CRYE Yes, I guess, and maybe a little money under the table...

Another strange thing was that while one would expect that these programs would be designed with soldiers, that soldiers would wear the gear and try everything out, it took us almost five months before we were able to test prototypes out on the users. And then it was done sort of illegally. We had U.S. Rangers test the gear, but under kind of behind-the-scenes conditions. There is so much red tape involved in using live test subjects that it's almost impossible to do informal design evaluations without completing a phonebook's worth of forms. So unfortunately, developers tend to avoid working directly with the users.

What is funny is that there's now a doll that's based on our system design. The Japanese apparently love army gear, and they make these twelve-inch-tall toys that are perfect replicas of soldiers. Sometimes they even make the toy gear better than we can actually make the real equipment. All the buckles work, the Velcro works, the zippers are real. They've copied our guy perfectly. We actually helped them copy it, because we thought it was so cool. And now even a video game is based on our design, so we keep getting phone calls from all these kooks...

VICTORE **What's it like working for the military? Do you get paid regularly?**

CRYE Well, it's funny; the military is this huge complex organization, and we actually only worked directly for the army for the first year on the project. It seems the army can't give the big projects to little guys. It's strange, but they just can't seem to force themselves to do it. So they give the big projects to large, familiar defense contractors, and now we work for several of these companies on this project. All I can say is that it's been a huge learning experience. We really enjoy and value the time we get to spend with the users, and we feel that we're contributing something that helps make their lives easier and helps protect them. But the business side of it is getting creepier and creepier and stranger and stranger.

FEHLBERG We've learned patience.

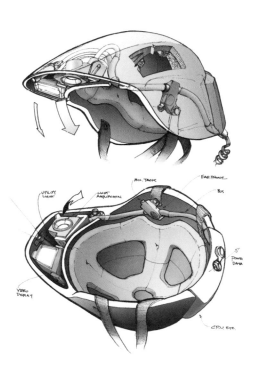

CRYE This is why we founded the production company Crye Precision. We started manufacturing and selling our gear ourselves (in Brooklyn), so that soldiers could get their hands on it and use it now. We were getting frustrated with how long it takes to develop something within such a bureaucratic system.

VICTORE **So soldiers can buy their own uniforms?**

CRYE They can buy their own.

Laughter

MCGUINNESS I'm going to talk a little bit about how we started working together. The 62 was initially founded to subvert the "post no bills" sections of pedestrian pathways. We wanted to get posters out there that would foster a dialogue rather than serve the predatory patter of advertisements. To appeal to a larger audience, we soon learned we had to work with clients. Employing a similar inquisitive and immediate voice and a simple style of xeroxing and collage, we began creating magazine and newspaper covers and cover inserts. We designed an insert for the *New York Press*, for example, and an insert about Critical Mass bike rides for a magazine called *Issue*, an art and culture magazine.

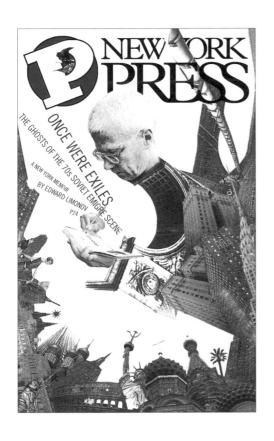

Critical Mass (originally known as "Commute Clot") was organized for the first time in San Francisco during the summer of 1992. The title was inspired by a line in Ted White's classic documentary *Return of the Scorcher*, where the term "Commute Clot" is used to describe traffic patterns in Beijing. During the 1890s, before roads were ruled by automobiles, cyclists where referred to as "scorchers" for their ability to reach such blazing speeds. Now, a century later, we have a world filled with car-related environmental and social problems. Critical Mass seeks to call attention to transportation alternatives. At The 62, we participate in Critical Mass bike rides because we want to promote a greener-minded transit. (Some studio mates have been arrested and prosecuted in the process.)

Grass Roots Urban Environmental Advocates. Mothers. Grandfathers. Social Workers. BMX Bandits. Stepchildren. Property Owners. The Handicapped. Skateboarders who will not see the Warner Brothers movie, Grind. A Republican, or Two. Journalists. Musicians. The Reverend Billy. Dogs. Connecticut Firemen. Curators. A Kid who has shopped at Urban Outfitters and got himself unlike Nas "a gun," but a Che Guevara T-shirt to fit in with...Squat Punks and Black Block. Fashion Photographers. Fast Food Deliverers. Yale Graduates. Members of The Puerto Rican Schwinn Club. A Ollin. A Card Carrying Communist from Eastern Europe. Advertisers. Nurses. Hipsters. Accountants. French People. Chic Fixed Gear Enthusiasts. Writers. Graffiti Writers. Construction Company Foremen. Tatooed People. Magazine Editors . Students . Police. Artists. LPR. Designers. House Painters. Carpenters. Educators. Some of the Hardest Working Non-Unionized Labor Force in Town. NYC Bike Messengers. Me and my Girlfriend who for one awaited night a month get to tour New York holding hands, riding bikes, side by side, our own version of a romantic cinematic cycle scene, engulfed n a projected hue, remembered predominately in 50's styled bubble gum era dresses sewn with poodles on them and wholesome, if not only in the idea, of those Campbells' soup kid's pink and blushing cheeks.

41

The notion of making posters and playing in the street also involves participating in demonstrations. We got involved in anti-war rallies, for example, and designed posters especially for these events. In 2002, somebody within the White House administration suggested that in an emergency situation people should tape and plaster their houses—their windows and all porous vents—with duct tape. They claimed that duct tape was going to save you in case of a nuclear or biological fallout. Our response to that was to create masks out of duct tape for a demonstration in New York City. We thought the masks would not only look good but also be great for protection against teargas. But the cops didn't like it, so we went back to making posters.

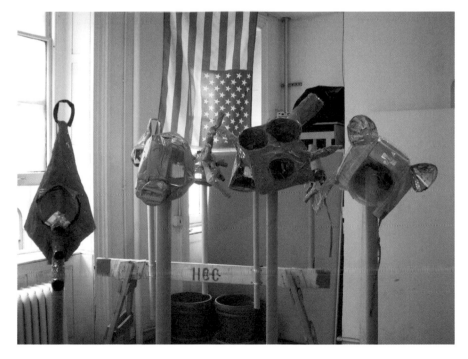

Andrei Kallaur designed a poster with Bush's head silkscreened atop a Pez dispenser. The spray paint-stenciled type reads "weapons of mass distraction." Our message was that Bush and his administration were candy-coating lies and feeding them to folks as if in time they wouldn't rot our world. I think we made at least a hundred of these posters, passing them out before a rally in Washington DC on October 23, 2002. It was well received, and lots of people gathered around to help post and carry the posters.

I also designed a poster for the Republican
Convention in 2004, which initially grew from a
xeroxed collage I had made of the Virgin Mary
holding two fingers extended to imply the "peace
sign," which to the European eye is a "fuck you"
sign. I wanted to visualize how conservative
America, with God on its side, was projecting
an Orwellian peace plot in order to wage war. I
thought it was a riot at first, but the image alone
did not have enough impact. So I turned the dial up
to eleven, kicked that ole "less is more" routine
to the curb, and put in more or less everything I
thought of the GOP.

VICTORE **Matt and Hubert, I'm going to ask you two to go backwards a little bit. Hubert, where did you go to school? What's your degree?**

MCCABE I have a couple of them. I have a degree in elementary education, a degree in American history with a specialization on foreign policy, and a clinical social work degree from New York University.

VICTORE **And Matthew?**

MCGUINNESS I graduated from the School of Visual Arts. I started off at the Rochester Institute of Technology. But it was too cold up there. And the skies were so grey. Plus, the snowball fights up there were relentless. So I moved down to New York. But my real motivation was to be where the action was. I wanted to get involved in global change and so forth; I wanted to play more in the streets. I graduated with a bachelor's degree in graphic design.

VICTORE **And then what came after that?**

MCGUINNESS Oh, I got a master's degree in social work too.

Laughter

No, after I graduated, I lived in Italy for a little while. I got an "Artist in Residency," so to speak, at a studio called Fabrica, founded by Oliviero Toscani, famous for his work for Benetton. Both Morgan Sheasby and I were at Fabrica.

VICTORE **The two of you went over?**

MCGUINNESS Yes, we worked together a lot and that was part of the reason why, after we came back to the States, we decided to continue working together. We wanted to establish our own Fabrica, so to speak, a studio workshop where people with like-minded ideas can get together.

CRYE Our next project doesn't have a home right now. We had the idea to develop an accessory for a handgun that would allow the gun to be shot only by its owner. We applied for a patent and started working on it, creating a computer model and a physical prototype.

The prototype works great and can be used with any kind of handgun. It basically consists of a ring and a special magazine that communicates with the ring. If the person holding the gun is wearing the correct ring, he can fire the gun, if he isn't wearing the ring, the gun doesn't fire. And you can't remove the magazine without having the ring.

We thought this kind of device would solve a big problem, giving police officers and homeowners the ability to secure their guns against unauthorized use. The problem is that no one seems eager to produce it—maybe because of the liability involved if it doesn't work. Recently, a suspect in Fulton County Courthouse was able to take a weapon from a police officer and shoot five people in the courtroom with the officer's weapon. This is the type of incident that our accessory is designed to prevent. The system physically works very well, now we're just trying to find a way to get it to work politically and commercially.

MCGUINNESS Our biggest project to date was Rebicycling, a collaborative arts project funded by the Bronx Museum of the Arts. For ten weeks, we worked with eight students from the Bronx International High School and the Highbridge Community Life Center, both located in the South Bronx, taking apart, rebuilding, stripping down, repainting, and redesigning old bicycles. (The Bicycle Station on Vanderbuilt Avenue in Brooklyn donated much-needed resources, and Carved Glass by Shefts in Hunts Point provided much-needed service.) While the students did most of the repair work themselves, we helped them come up with identities or a title for their artwork (or what is commonly referred to as a bike). One girl, for example, dedicated her bike to all the people that had passed away in the course of her life. Somebody else had a knack for the environment, so she named her bike Nature Lover. Another person named the bike after himself.

MCCABE We worked in the lobby of the Bronx Museum, hanging out, cooking lunch or dinner for each other, blasting music. We had a great time. At the end of the ten weeks, everybody rode away with their own bikes, which they had created. While we were there, Rebicycling was a sort of ongoing exhibition at the museum. Now, all that's left are photos. And the magazine *The Good Apple* published an article with a series of spreads on the project.

MCGUINNESS Recycle-a-Bicycle, which has offices in Manhattan, Brooklyn, and now the South Bronx, actually does a very like-minded project, but they don't integrate all of the same values that we were trying to get across. Rebicycling involved educational workshops on issues such as cycling, health, transportation, and alternative life styles. We also did poetry readings and experimental drawing collectives to get the kids engaged while they were eating lunch.

After the project, we donated all our tools and with the Bronx Museum resources helped to establish a Recycle-a-Bicycle in the local community so that our project did not just leave after its ten-week run. They orchestrated a space in a neighboring high school and continue to refurbish used bicycles for the South Bronx.

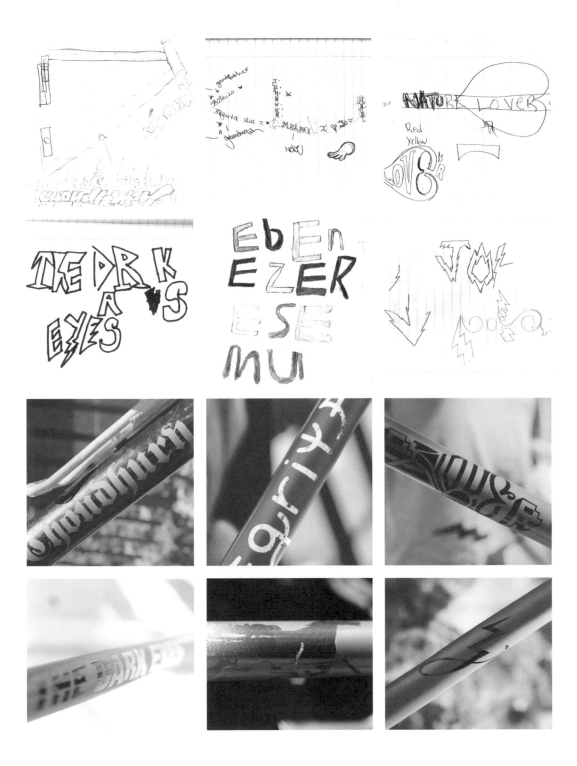

MCCABE We went back about a month ago to distribute copies of the magazine with the article on Rebicycling to the kids. Most of them still had their bikes, and most of them were still riding. Others had crashed their bikes or been hit by cars. But they were all very excited to see us, which was really nice. It demonstrated that you can work in the community and have a lasting effect beyond what you thought possible. Everybody was telling stories: "Do you remember when we did this? Do you ever see this person any more? Is there any chance we're going to be able to do it again?," and so on and so forth.

MCGUINNESS It was a very rewarding project.

VICTORE **So wait a minute. Are any of you guys graphic designers?**

MCCABE Well, three of us have graphic design degrees.

VICTORE **Caleb? Eric? Are you graphic designers?**

CRYE No.

VICTORE **No? A little bit?**

CRYE No. But we do all of our own graphic design. Does that count?

Last year we were hired by Lion Apparel, the leading producer of what is called "bunker gear" or "turnout gear"—basically fire-retardant suits for firemen. They'd seen the military work we'd done and asked us to help them design a new and better fire-fighting suit. This was a pretty short project because there was a tight timeline. It was actually nice to have just one single piece of gear to design—very simple and clean, not too complicated.

FEHLBERG It's very discreet compared to the military equipment.

VICTORE **What were the problems they were having with the old suits?**

FEHLBERG Mainly, they were too bulky and limiting. We redesigned the suits from the ground up so they'd provide the needed insulation but fit a lot better, move better, and be less restrictive. We also wanted to make them more protective. Because even though the old suits were fireproof, there were places where fire fighters would always get burned by water and steam. Protective suits are often designed—and we found this was true for the army too—on a mannequin that's standing up while in reality people who are wearing protective apparel are moving and active in their environment. The firemen, for example, complained that they kept getting burned not from the fire but from burning water, almost boiling water, that comes in at their legs when they're crawling. It turns out the suits were never designed for crawling. So we designed our suit so that water can't get in when you're crawling. We had to really question the firemen to find out what needed to be fixed. They didn't tell us about the burning water, for example, until we had had several meetings with them. They just get used to these kinds of problems and won't even complain about them.

The final production version of the suit differs somewhat from the prototype, as there're always a few little compromises you need to make whenever you go from a prototype to production. But I always think the production version is so much cooler because it's real.

VICTORE **So are the firemen going to be using these? How soon?**

FEHLBERG They're already using them.

VICTORE **And you started working on the military gear in 2000, and they're going to use it in 2010?**

FEHLBERG That's correct. There's a lot of bureaucracy.

FEHLBERG The next project we worked on was a redesign of an exoskeleton that DARPA had developed.

VICTORE **Can you tell us who they are? DARPA?**

FEHLBERG DARPA is the Defense Advanced Research Project Agency. Even though it's a defense agency, I think they're part of the Department of Energy. They're huge and have a lot of money to spend on thinking up crazy ideas such as robots that drive themselves across the country.

CRYE They're part of the illuminati.

Laughter

VICTORE **Making those $500 toilet seats...**

FEHLBERG Exactly. The $500,000 toilet seats and the GPS system. They also invented the Internet—not Al Gore-style, they really did invent it. Anyway, DARPA had developed an exoskeleton, but they wanted it to look better and integrate better with the wearer. We were commissioned to design a kind of skin for it. It was a fun little project because the engineers had been working on the mechanism for almost five years, and then we came along and in a few weeks developed the skin that covers it all up.

CRYE They didn't like that.

Laughter

FEHLBERG Yeah, they weren't fans. Now, whenever anybody sees it, they see our enclosure design and not the mechanism the engineers have been sweating over for their entire lifetime.

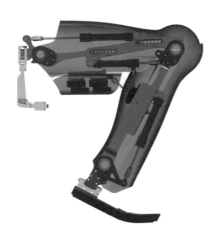

The Future Soldier is another design project for the army. It's basically science fiction: we were asked to design the soldier of the year 2020. Because this is so far into the future, the design was mostly guesswork.

CRYE The army gave us a list of things that they thought would be developed by then, and in addition asked us to make up a bunch of other stuff too. So the Future Soldier has got these random electro-gizmos everywhere that represent sensors or detectors or something.

Laughter

VICTORE **So in 2020, these are the cops that'll be stopping Critical Mass bike rides?**

Laughter

MCGUINNESS We've collaborated on a number of projects
with a nonprofit organization called Conjunction
Arts. Their goal is to put artists who make or
would like to make public artworks in touch with
like-minded organizations or corporations that
have the money to facilitate the ideas of these
artists. One of these projects was an artwork by
Bradley McCallum and Jacqueline Tarry. It was
called *Silence* and involved mapping the underground
railroad in certain locations in the northern
states to call into question contemporary race
relations. In 2001 my friend Francesca Jaccia and I
got involved in *Silence*, working together with the
artists on a site in New Haven, Connecticut.

During the 1800s, an all-black congregation
had split off from the originally mixed-race Center
Church in New Haven and started their own church
called Dixwell Avenue Church because they were not
allowed to sit in the lower level of the church
together with the white parishioners and also
suffered other forms of discrimination. The two
churches still exist today, and the present-day
church communities are trying to talk about their
relationship and history. The two pastors have
traded places, for example, giving lectures to each
other's congregation.

In *Silence* we commemorated the eighteen
people who first left the church, making headstone-
like epitaphs with samples of language we found
inscribed on plaques throughout the lower level
of the church. Our work was exhibited at Center
Church, but the church's Board of Stewards, a
governing body responsible for maintenance and use
of the church, elected to remove portions of the
artwork; specifically, the photographs of Dixwell
Avenue congregation members were moved from the
central seating area and placed in the balcony.
The artists, in a public statement declared, that
"the actions of the Board of Stewards to remove
the artwork, prompted by private lobbying of
parishioners, without notifying the Pastors, the
congregation, the sponsoring arts organization, or
the artists, is an example of history repeating
itself."

MEMBER Nº
1828

In Memory of
MARIA RAYMOND
.COLORED.

Dismissed to the African Church, August of the 18th year of this age, faithful to her convictions of duty earnest in an age of controversy, born into freedom she was active, strong and ambitious.

Another site-specific project that was part of *Silence* was a sculpture called *Looking For...*, which was created for the Neuberger Sculpture Biennial, taking place on the five-hundred-acre sculpture grounds just outside SUNY-Purchase in Westchester County. One of the major landowners there during the time of the underground railroad and abolition was a family called the Thomases. Their old land now makes up most of the sculpture grounds at SUNY-Purchase. Even though the Thomases owned slaves, they were still among the most highly respected families around at that time. Apparently, a lot of whites still had slaves in the North then, which I hadn't realized. When we tried to learn more about this particular family legacy, we found out that the Thomas family burial ground also contained that of their slaves, though their graves were unmarked.

Brad and Jacqueline had the idea to celebrate those whose deaths were disremembered, so we hired somebody to take ultrasound photographs of the ground to find spots that were presumably remnants of bodies. Brad and Jacqueline built headstones, which showed the ultrasound photograph of a possible corpse underground, for those spots, and we built a gate at the entrance to the cemetery to commemorate the slaves that the Thomas family had owned. A plaque on the gate recounts the history of these slaves. The bodies buried inside were those of two boys, two girls, a woman servant, and an elder servant who survived the family but was sold rather than freed. On the other side of the gate another slave is commemorated: as you leave the cemetery, you can read about one gentleman, called Jim, who managed to escape. It's not known how he escaped but the records suggest that he did. Exiting the grounds, you get the same view of the fields that Jim would have had, and you can imagine the courage and dedication it must have taken him to flee.

69

VICTORE **How was the gate made?**

MCGUINNESS It was fabricated in a small studio in Baltimore. I don't know very much about how it was done. It's water jet-cut with laser precision. Apparently this works similar to a vinyl cutter.

VICTORE **What were the plaques inside made of?**

MCGUINNESS I think they were photographs laminated on aluminum. They were archival, but I believe only the gate will be in the permanent collection.

VICTORE **Tell me about the doorknob of the gate.**

MCGUINNESS The doorknob spells out our sexy logo. That was our contribution. It's a six on one side and a two on the other side.

CRYE After we did the exoskeleton design for them, DARPA hired us for another project, which had to do with urban combat. They were looking for ideas on how to help military personnel keep buildings that they've cleared, clear.

Our first proposals centered around how glue could be used to inhibit human traffic or to indicate whether structure had been re-occupied. We thought that using glue to make barriers would be fun, but the kinds we would probably have ended up using are fairly toxic, so luckily DARPA picked another one of our concepts to pursue. The final design was a barrier out of razor barbed wire that can be made on the spot. Normally, people who handle barbed wire and other types of military barrier material have to wear thick gloves, and they still end up getting cut. In other words, they don't like it, and they don't want to carry it around. So we decided to develop a machine that makes this kind of barrier material on the spot. Using this machine, you can make a big mess out of barbed wire and then leave it in a stairwell or hallway to prevent people from entering the building.

FEHLBERG The machine we designed is really heavy, but it works very well. There're two rolling dyes that cut out the barbed-wire shape where they meet. There's also a device that puts a crease in the wire, which gives it some strength. Another piece chomps the wire and gives it a coil. Scott, our main engineer on the project, tested it first and he actually got tangled up in it by mistake and cut himself quite badly... But no hard feelings.

Laughter

CRYE We had no idea if such a machine would even work. That's what's nice about working for DARPA—they don't know if it'll work, they're just trying to figure stuff out. They didn't know if the exoskeleton would work either. But they wanted to be the first ones to figure out whether it's possible.

Anyway, the future home for this machine is probably embassies. It will enable the Marines who guard embassies to quickly enclose the place if angry mobs are approaching, without having the building look like an overly guarded institution.

VICTORE **You know, my sister lives in a gated community. They could probably use this too.**

FEHLBERG Yes, I'm pretty sure "Ridgecrest Meadows" ordered a couple.

Laughter

74

Another project we did for DARPA developed out of their need to climb on top of buildings without using a ladder. Our design grew out of the glue ideas that we'd been working on at the beginning of the barbed wire project. We developed small steps that could be glued to the outside of a building and tested all the different kinds of glues that you could use for this purpose. The fastest and strongest one turned out to be hot glue.

VICTORE **Craft glue?**

CRYE Yes, like Martha Stewart hot glue.

FEHLBERG Caleb tested the prototype, actually walking up a forty-five-foot-tall building.

CRYE They made me try it out first, because I was the one who said it would work, while everyone kept saying, "No, it'll never work." It was a pretty scary experience. You glue the step on and hold it there and clip a safety line to it. After about forty seconds, you unhook the safety line from the step you had previously glued on and put all of your weight on the new one. For the first ten feet or so, you don't really care. But after about thirty or forty feet, you really don't want to lean back on this thing you just hot-glued to the wall.

Laughter

FEHLBERG It was funny, because it would creak or make little sounds.

CRYE Bad sounds.

FEHLBERG And Caleb was up there, and he would say, "It's making terrible noises." But it actually worked. You can essentially climb any size wall that you're brave enough to climb, because you can carry as many of these steps as you can fit into your backpack. Whereas with a ladder, you essentially can't climb higher than its length.

VICTORE **Is DARPA going to use this?**

CRYE They're shopping it around but there are no takers yet.

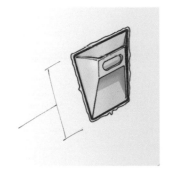

MCCABE Our most recent project grew out of our tradition to invite everybody we know to join us to go sleigh riding in Fort Greene Park in Brooklyn on the first day of serious snow every year. The catch is that we make all the sleds ourselves out of trash. When the weather gets cold each fall, we start collecting everything that we think might make a good sled. And when we know there's going to be a good snowstorm, we all get together in Andrei's basement and start drilling all these things together. Eventually, more and more people show up, and we all go to Fort Greene Park, where we have a huge party, riding down the hill and breaking all the sleds that took us hours to build.

In late 2004, we received a call for proposals from Exit Art on Thirty-sixth Street and Tenth Avenue for a show called "Other America." We sent them the sleigh-riding idea, designing a really nice little book with photos and a sketch illustrating it. At first, they said, "we don't get it. Is it a performance piece, is it a sculpture project, is it going to be open to the public?"

MCGUINNESS "Is it just this drawing?"

MCCABE We said, "It's all these things." They liked the idea a lot, and so we built a ten-foot-high ramp in the main gallery at Exit Art. The ramp included a "bump," because their insurance wouldn't allow us to call it a jump. So we had a bump.

Laughter

78

We fabricated our own OSHA safety devices with the help of our friends Allison Corrie and Leslie Stem, putting larger-than-life stuffed animals such as a mole, a fish with trailing excrement, a porcupine, and a walrus on top of twenty or so foam-filled pillows.

MCCABE So we would come launching off the top on one of our self-built sleds, hit the bump, and land in our interpretations of Dr. Seuss's Lorax. Alongside, we put up tires for psychological safety.

MCGUINNESS Working with Exit Art was great, because they basically let us do everything we wanted. At the opening, there were some 1,000 people, and they let us not only ride the ramp ourselves but also every visitor who wanted to. We ended up having a line stretching through the whole huge gallery with everybody who was there. Little kids, people with fancy shoes—everybody wanted to try it. They would all ride down the ramp and get a huge kick out of it. The installation was up for about three months at Exit Art. Initially, the sleigh-riding was supposed to take place only on Saturdays, but we found out that the staff would be doing it on Mondays when they got in. So we'd come in on Saturdays and would have to rebuild the whole thing because it was all broken.

MCCABE But mostly we broke it ourselves.

MCGUINNESS Every Saturday, we went to the gallery, and people would start showing up; all our friends would come, people who had heard about it, and people who were traveling through town would show up. So we all went sledding throughout the whole spring. It was great.

Influences

VICTORE **Now that we saw examples of your work, I'm interested to know what runs you guys, what's behind all these projects, what keeps you going. Caleb and Eric, do you love what you do?**

CRYE Absolutely. I love working on projects where we don't know how they're going to turn out. It keeps you up at night but it's also challenging and motivating. We've been in business for a little over five years, and it's fun to look back because many of the ideas that seemed so scary at the beginning turned out pretty good.

FEHLBERG With some of the projects, it doesn't really matter that much if they don't work. But in other cases, the consequences can be very serious. People can die or get badly hurt.

VICTORE **Designers like to joke around, "Hey! It ain't brain surgery. No one's going to get hurt." How do you deal with the fact that not only people may end up getting hurt but the U.S. military is going to continually put our boys in really shitty situations?**

CRYE Well, it's something that we just take on. We kind of wish more of the design community would take on such responsibility. I think lawyers—I hope there're no lawyers here tonight—have, generally speaking, created an environment where people are afraid to do anything innovative for fear of being sued if someone gets hurt using a new design; especially with safety equipment. But so far, our users have really appreciated what we did for them. They actually want something that's better, whether or not someone may end up getting hurt in it. That's most likely going to happen. But you're never going to get any progress unless you're willing to invest in a project and put your name on it and say, "I think this is going to help people and I'm going to stand behind it."

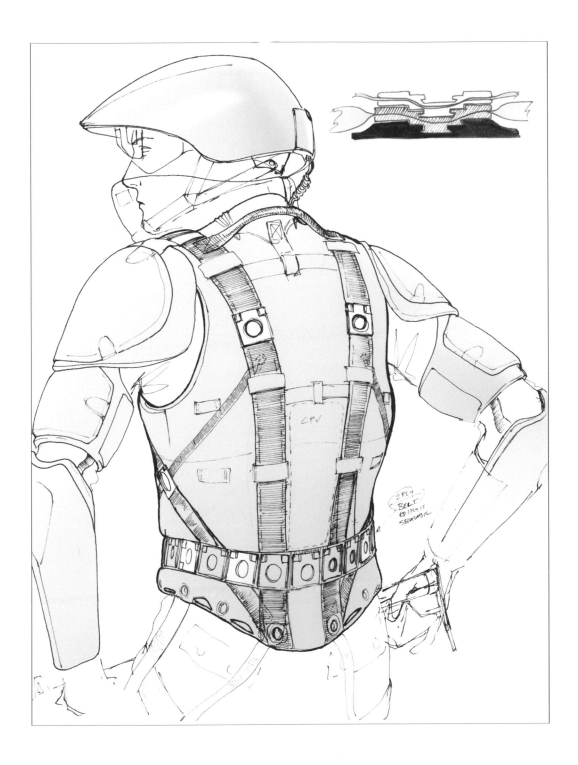

VICTORE **You started most of these projects in 2000, and for all of Crye Associates's life, you've been working under a Bush administration. So, is it "It's my country, right or wrong"? Or are there things you don't do? Would not do?**

CRYE Our professional ethics are fairly consistent among our staff but we do have a lot of different political views. The main thing for us, though, is that we're very committed to our work and feel that what we're doing is helping our guys. Politically, there're some things we agree with and some things we don't. But we always focus on helping the actual individuals we work with. Because they are the ones who use the stuff, and it literally helps keep them alive. I feel indebted to them. I wouldn't want to have anything to do with their working environment. The sacrifices they make and the professionalism they are able to maintain in some of the worst conditions imaginable are just amazing. They're making these big sacrifices essentially for *me* and anyone else, and this really inspires me to work with and for them.

VICTORE **What is The 62 influenced by?**

MCGUINNESS I'm often inspired by things I see in my everyday life. For example, this truck here, which had changed the signs that usually say PASS on the left and DO NOT PASS on the right, to AMERICANS and TERRORISTS. Morgan and I were driving directly behind the truck, which had stalled, and thought this was hilarious. A line of honking cars formed behind us, and we passed on the right in order not to miss another green light. I actually used to be a tractor-trailer truck driver myself.

MCCABE Not used to. Recently.

MCGUINNESS It's true; between art and design gigs, I sometimes work as a truck driver. When I was a kid in high school, I took an advanced placement test, which concluded that my bread would be buttered from diesel and dust. I was in a prep school, and kids where going on to national hockey, international law, and the Catholic parish. My fate: the cockpit of eighteen steel wheels. I was excited, though; I thought, what could be more American working class—how romantic. But as they say, love is a word used by the young to describe what is really lust. Still, trucking allowed me to converse with folks I would never have met otherwise. And sometimes I find that the truck driving business, despite its conservative bend, provides for a more liberal tongue.

But in the end, I decided that if I had to be starving, I'd rather be a starving artist than a starving tractor-truck driver. The 62 is a labor of love. It's an extracurricular activity, so to speak. We do this at nighttime, and we don't really make that much money with it. If we do make money, it's more like a stipend, if anything.

VICTORE **In one of the conversations we've had, Caleb used the phrase "industrial optimist." Would you call yourself an "industrial optimist"?**

CRYE Yes, if there were an Industrial Optimist Society, I'd be a card-carrying member. Basically, our whole company is based on the idea that we were put on this earth to use our ability to think and create to do just that—to think and create. Sometimes that takes crazy tangents like the flying car contraption shown here, and other times it gives us things like language and electricity. People are still working on the flying car. I don't know why. It doesn't make sense to me. But we're fascinated by things that are right on the edge of failure. I'm always drawn to concepts like the flying car because it's based on the same mindset that created the light bulb—this fundamental instinct to believe that something you've imagined is possible and that, if you can just figure it out, you can make it become real. The flying car instinct eventually gave us the airliner and space travel. So a lot of the photographs we're going to look at here show things that impress us and are just good reference points for us.

MCGUINNESS I guess I'm just the opposite. If Caleb is a member of the Industrial Optimists, then I'd be a card-carrying member of the Industrial Pessimists Club. Caleb was talking about the idea of progress, the creative spark, and the notion that we're on some sort of track that's going somewhere. Well, I agree with all that, but I'm not quite sure whether it's the right track.

VICTORE **E. E. Cummings calls progress a comfortable disease.**

MCGUINNESS Well, I think that just because something is electronic doesn't mean it's necessarily better. Where Caleb sees a flying car, I see the Staten Island landfill. One of the things that we're trying to do in The 62 is to take our responsibility as graphic designers seriously. Many of the things graphic designers create, such as leaflets or catalogs and so on, eventually end up in landfills. So for this event tonight we worked together with the printer Greg Barber on producing the invitations. They're 100 percent post-consumer: the material is reused, and we used soy inks. So you can almost feel good about throwing it out.

VICTORE **Hey, Matt. People don't throw my stuff away.**

Laughter

MCGUINNESS Anyway, to get back to the quote you mentioned, I think progress is a really uncomfortable disease.

CRYE For us, the point is that you've got to believe in something. What impresses us as a company and me in particular is the ability of humans to interact with their world in a way that creates something and out of nothing generates meaning, beauty, and utility. That's what I consider to be progress. We're all monkeys, but we're the monkeys with tools. We're the only living beings who can change our world to make it better suit us. I think of it as life trying to figure itself out through us, and I think it's an incredibly noble goal to try to help that. And I believe that's our only job—to help life figure itself out. Sometimes you get a useless contraption in the process, sometimes you get something amazing.

MCGUINNESS Sometimes you get a lot of garbage.

CRYE Sometimes you get a whole lot of garbage. The fact is, most of the time you get a whole lot of garbage but from that big pile of garbage, every now and then you get a cure for a disease or the concept of language, or you get the light bulb or agriculture.

FEHLBERG Or the Ducati 916.

CRYE The most perfect motorcycle ever made.

Laughter

It's out of date now. There're faster motorcycles around but there's never been one that is such a perfect marriage of form and function and simplicity and elegance.

MCGUINNESS This is a replica of a bicycle, called the Safety Cycle, which was fabricated around the turn of the century, when bicycling became popular. A bike was a little bit easier than a horse to maintain, and it wasn't as expensive as the train.

VICTORE **Whose bike is this?**

MCGUINNESS It belonged to a gentleman by the name of Major Taylor who's probably one of the most amazing American athletes we have to date. At the turn of the century, cycling was at its peak, but Major Taylor was absolutely radical. He was a black athlete, and the best in his game. Reading his biography, you find that he didn't win because he was just fast. He won because he was afraid the other guys were going to lynch him if they caught up with him. So he won a lot of money by getting away from his enemies. For me, this bicycle represents the ability to overcome both bureaucratic and physical opposition. It reminds me of a terrible time in our nation's history, when a man, against all immeasurable odds, rose to the title of hero.

VICTORE **Why is your studio called The 62?**

MCCABE It is kind of a throwback to the tradition of graffiti writers who take the name of the street they live in to demark their identity. Some writers use the word "one" as a kind of surname, implying the one and only, an individual, but many others take their respective street number or address, steeped in the pride of being from a particular place. Our studio is at 62 Washington Avenue, but our name also involves other ideas. Sixty-two miles above the Earth's surface is where space starts, and we like to think that that's where we play. And every 62 billion years the Earth goes through a regenerative process; everything becomes extinct. We're 63 billion years into this regenerative process, so we're one billion years overdue for an extinction.

VICTORE **You should have moved a couple of doors down the other side of the street. Could have been 69.**

From the work we saw before, I get an idea of what you make financially. So my question is: When are you going to start earning something? When are you going to get a job? When are you going to start paying rent?

MCGUINNESS I'm on that path. I recently cut my hair... What we make? We didn't make very much last year. I think it was around $10,000, tops, for The 62.

VICTORE **I asked Caleb and Eric earlier where they would draw the line. How about you guys at The 62? What wouldn't you do? What won't you do? Would you do cigarettes, for example?**

MCGUINNESS I've done cigarettes. I mean, I have a day job, too. I don't live on $10,000. Although that would be a good project...

But there're things you have to take care of, bills you have to pay. Today is the way today works, and I do take jobs. I was a tractor-trailer truck driver. I was a bike messenger. I've been a house painter. And I work in advertising agencies large and small. I pretty much do it all. Well, obviously, there is stuff I wouldn't do.

VICTORE **Like what?**

MCGUINNESS I don't know. Coke. Cocaine. Slave trade.
It's a complex question. I don't know what I really
wouldn't do. I thought once, when I was younger,
that I would never do cigarettes. But you know,
I recently designed the hell out of cigarette
packs, made the best-looking ones. I'll go back
to smoking in a minute when these things hit the
market. (I don't know if they are.) And I know that
what I'm doing is not fair and cool, and it's not
what I really want to do or where I want to be in
the world. But I haven't gotten to that place yet
where I can choose. So that's what The 62 is. It's
a bunch of friends saying, "Okay, in real life,
unfortunately, we have to work. That sucks. But
in this company at least, let's do something that
we really believe in. Even if it will never pay
the bills."

VICTORE **Wait. Do any of you guys smoke?**

MCGUINNESS Sometimes I smoke.

VICTORE **So, what's the big deal?**

MCGUINNESS Well, I just don't think it's a healthy
lifestyle, and I don't want to contribute to making
a new smoker out of anybody.

MCCABE I think it also goes back to what Caleb said
earlier. We all have these talents and gifts, and
we'd rather use them for something we can stand
behind than for cigarette advertising.

VICTORE **Caleb and Eric. Do you have a military background in your families?**

CRYE My Dad was a Marine. But I have never been in the service.

FEHLBERG I was raised a liberal in Canada. My parents are shocked and dismayed by what I do.

VICTORE **Caleb, tell me about this picture.**

CRYE This is one of my favorite images. I think going to the moon was, although useless for a lot of reasons, probably the coolest thing that humans have ever done. We're the animals that took ourselves to the moon. That's what we're all about, as far as I'm concerned— this push, this drive to test our limits. The image shows astronaut John W. Young collecting rock samples. What is amazing is that the tool he uses is basically just a hammer. It may be a very expensive hammer (probably a $500 DARPA hammer), but essentially it's the same tool that's been around since the beginning of human history.
    The hammer fundamentally solves a problem in a perfect form. It's simple. It's elegant. It's all you need. And there's no reason even on the moon for there to be a different hammer. It's essentially the same tool that Og made in prehistoric times. It's also an inspiration for us to build on the advancements of others. This man is on the moon using a hammer as a direct result of the invention of the hammer itself. This first human tool literally made possible each subsequent development, which eventually got us to space.

MCGUINNESS While Morgan and I were living in Italy, the G8 summit took place in Genoa. We decided to organize a workshop at Fabrica, because we found that many residents didn't really understand what the G8 was and why the great nations of the world were gathering there in Italy. We wanted to heighten their awareness by having them design posters with some sort of social commentary or question.

As we were developing the workshop, Morgan and I decided that we should all go to Genoa and take part in the protest with the posters we made. We had the idea of putting several posters together to create one big image. The complete poster would be carried by eight people. Each person would hold an individual poster, and seen together they would form the complete image, similar to a Chinese dragon. We wanted to achieve the same celebratory parade atmosphere.

In each of the individual sections or posters appears a portrait of one of the G8 leaders. These portraits are connected by key chains to a kind of machine we fabricated out of industrial tractor and car parts, pipes, and pumps. One section is fused together with bicycle parts. We used that one as a platform for Bush's portrait and got a kick out of it, because obviously bicycling is not part of his platform. The machine in its impossible and absurd nature reminded us of the convoluted construct in the movie *Brazil.* One can visualize this machine and its agriculture-tilling properties tearing up and changing the face of the earth, leaking oil right into the ground because of its many old and worn-out connections.

We took part in the protest, running away from what seemed to be Crye's future soldier designs in action. Later, we found that much of what happened during the demonstrations was omitted by the mainstream press. It was quite possibly the most overpoweringly oppressive display of power I have ever witnessed. But this experience, the workshop as well as taking part in the demonstration, was a great influence on us and played a role in our decision to found The 62.

VICTORE **Do you guys believe in changing the world?**

MCGUINNESS I think ultimately that's why we get together and do what we do. At the end of the day we want to try and build a better life for everybody.

George W. Bush ℞ / ᵗᴴ

FEHLBERG The Lockheed SS71 Blackbird is the coolest airplane ever made. It's also the fastest plane ever built; it goes 3,000 miles per hour. It almost doesn't work. It gets so hot when it flies that it has to be held together loosely when it's on the ground. Until it gets up to speed, it's leaking and rattling and barely working. The pilots have to wear space suits, and the glass of the cockpit heats up to the point that you can't touch it. It's an amazingly difficult object to design—again an example of people going to the edge of what's possible, producing something that you'd never think could ever work.

CRYE And not to forget that this was designed in a one-year time frame, 1968, without the use of computers.

VICTORE **Hey! You know what I was just thinking? You guys would make an ass-kicking sled.**

CRYE You bet.

Laughter

We've already reserved space at the next 62 sled day.

VICTORE **The 62, why the graffiti?**

MCGUINNESS Graffiti for us is a good example of the do-it-yourself philosophy that our company is based on.

VICTORE **But you don't do graffiti? Right? That's illegal.**

MCGUINNESS No, no, no. Just talking from an observer's point of view.

VICTORE **It's interesting to see these slides of graffiti after we saw the camouflage project earlier.**

MCGUINNESS I really like this guy's graffiti. I think he's not alive anymore. He was very prolific, very political, getting out there, trying to get kids to read books and talk about God and so forth. Apparently, he used to be an English teacher. People like him have always been an inspiration for me.

CRYE This is a weird kind of lettuce plant. What I like about this image is that you can clearly see the rules based on which this plant is generated. There are all these hidden forces in the world. As designers, as physical designers, our job is pretty much to understand those forces, work within them, and create something that utilizes them. You can't fight these forces. You can't win against gravity. You can't win against the second law of thermodynamics.

VICTORE **This is not a cross between cauliflower and something else?**

CRYE No. This is just how the plant exists. It's nature giving you a math lesson.

FEHLBERG Yes, it's basically a perfect fractal pattern.

VICTORE **Can you eat it?**

CRYE You can eat it.

MCGUINNESS This is Brooklyn's very own Cyclone, made of wood. We wanted our sledding project to emulate the fear and anxiety that you feel just before you drop down your first hill on the Cyclone. And I think we were successful. The folks who run the Cyclone came to the show and rode the sled, and they were really impressed.

MCGUINNESS Taking part in protests is important for us at The 62. A long time ago, I met a gentleman who had participated in the civil rights movement in the South. I thought how changed our world was, due in part to his struggle and that of others elsewhere throughout our country. The 62, at times large and small, have advertised and provided alternative ideas, from cycling to sledding and farming to statesmanship. Sometimes we party, sometimes we political-party. "To sin by silence when they should protest makes cowards of men," as Abraham Lincoln said.

CRYE FedEx is one of my favorite companies. It's an incredible success story about a guy who started out with a crazy idea. No one would invest in him. No one believed in him. Today, his company owns over 1,000 planes and even delivers a big chunk of the U.S. mail for the Post Office. A truly impressive story. And at the same time, FedEx constantly operates on the verge of failure. All of these planes have to deliver huge volumes of stuff in tiny amounts of time, and sometimes the planes crash. But this is part of what the company is willing to deal with and accept. Luckily, the crew usually gets out. In this case, they did. But they lost a lot of packages.

VICTORE **Is that where it went? I've been waiting for fucking three weeks for that thing.**

Laughter

CRYE So what this picture shows is that if you're going to push the edge, you've got to be ready for failure as well.

118

CRYE I chose this picture of the American flag on the moon, because I think the idea of America deserves more respect than it usually receives. I believe in this place and its role; with its imperfect democracy and capitalism, it's pretty much the most authentic human civilization that has ever been devised. It definitely has a lot of problems. But it at least allows for human creativity and ingenuity. And, to be honest, in our society today, creativity is really all we've got left to export, since we don't produce much here anymore. Creativity is the thing we give the world—our media, our designs, and our stories.

MCGUINNESS This piece is part of a larger project we've been doing. We take the base plates of lampposts off, design them, decorate them, and put them back on.

VICTORE **You've been doing that?**

MCGUINNESS Yes, and we started passing the idea on to other designers as well.

VICTORE **What size hex wrench do you need to take those off?**

MCGUINNESS I forget the size. But that's okay because otherwise you'd all be doing this. This particular one I thought was especially appropriate for our times. The symbol illustrated is a hand gesture from sign language that means "love." I find this image a fitting background to what Caleb said earlier about admiring the idea of America despite its failures. Tonight we are shaking up the black-and-white rhetoric, all the polarizing shit that usually just ends up getting in the way of having a real conversation and dealing with problems. The right-or-wrong, black-and-white all around us, we want to make it gray and provide a point for inspiration and love. It's a lot of work, especially if redecorating city lampposts is your labor, and there's only so much one can do alone. But together, we are so dynamic and diverse, capable of so many things, and can learn so much from each other.

VICTORE **On that note, we are going to call it quits for this evening. Thank you very much for coming. Good night.**

Applause

Music/
background
conversation

122

Project Credits

19 top: Crye Associates, logo, 2001; designers: Crye
Associates

19 bottom: The 62, logo, 2002; designers: The 62

21 top: soldier wearing MultiCam™ in desert surroundings,
2003; photo: Caleb Crye, Crye Associates

21 bottom: MultiCam™, early versions, 2002; designers: Crye
Associates; client: U.S. Army

23: MultiCam™, final version, 2003; designers: Crye
Associates

25: soldier wearing MultiCam™ standing in front of wall,
2003; photo: Crye Associates

27 top, middle: Fourtealizer illustrations, 2003; venue:
Renewable Brooklyn; designer: Matthew McGuinness, The 62

27 bottom left, right: Fourtealizer illustrations, 2003;
venue: Renewable Brooklyn; designer: Morgan Sheasby, The
62

29 top left: Future Ec(h)os, exhibition detail, 2003; venue:
Renewable Brooklyn; designers and photography: The 62;
private collection

29 top right: Fourtealizer illustration, 2003; venue:
Renewable Brooklyn; designer: Andrei Kallaur, The 62

29 bottom: Future Ec(h)os, exhibition detail, 2003; venue:
Renewable Brooklyn; designers and photography: The 62;
private collection

31 top: Future Force Warrior with gun, photo, 2004;
designers and photography: Crye Associates; client: U.S.
Army

31 bottom left: Future Force Warrior vest, prototype, 2004;
designers and photography: Crye Associates; client: U.S.
Army

31 bottom right: Future Force Warrior vest, model, 2003;
designers: Crye Associates; client: U.S. Army

33 Future Force Warrior, early concept illustrations, 2001,
designers: Crye Associates; client: U.S. Army

35 top left: Future Force Warrior, early concept, 2002;
designers: Crye Associates; client: U.S. Army

35 top right: Future Force Warrior helmet, rendering, 2001;
designers: Crye Associates; client: U.S. Army

35 bottom left: Future Force Warrior helmet, early concept,
2001; designers: Crye Associates; client: U.S. Army

35 bottom right: Future Force Warrior helmet, final model,
2001; designers: Crye Associates; client: U.S. Army

37 top: Advanced Combat Uniform, 2004; photography: U.S.
Army, Crye Associates; client: U.S. Army

37 bottom: Future Force Warrior rifle, 2003; designers: Crye
Associates; client: U.S. Army

39 top: Knox Overstreet, poster, silkscreen, 2002;
designers: Matthew McGuinness and Andrei Kallaur, The
62; photography: The 62

39 bottom left: *New York Press* cover, 2003; designers:
Andrei Kallaur and Morgan Sheasby, The 62; creative
director: Nick Bilton

39 bottom right: *New York Press* cover insert, 2003;

designers: Matthew McGuinness and Morgan Sheasby, The 62; creative director: Nick Bilton

41: *Do You Know Where We are Going: A Critical Mass Story*, 2004; designer, author, and illustrator: Matthew McGuiness

43: Art During War Time, Biological Weapons/Tear Gas Masks, 2004; designers/protesters: The 62; photography: The 62

45 top: Weapons of Mass Distraction, poster, 2003; designer: Andrei Kallaur, The 62

45 bottom: October 26 anti-war protest, Washington DC, 2003; photographer: Matthew McGuinness

47: poster, 2005; publisher: Please Post, RNC Issue; designer: Matthew McGuinness, The 62

49: Knox Overstreet, poster, silkscreen, 2002; designers: Matthew McGuinness and Andrei Kallaur, The 62

51 top: handgun accessory, prototype, 2004; designers: Crye Associates; photography: Rob DeSaint-Phaille

51 bottom left: handgun accessory, rendering, 2004; designers: Crye Associates

51 bottom right: handgun accessory, prototype, 2004; designers: Crye Associates; photography: Scott Thompson

53: Invitation for Rebicycling, 2004; exhibition space: Bronx Museum of the Arts; artists: The 62

55: Detail of spread in *The Good Apple*, Rebicycling, 2004; designers: The 62; photography: The 62

57 top: Rebicycling, 2004; exhibition space: Bronx Museum of The Arts; artist: The 62; photography: The 62

57 bottom: Carlos, Rebicycling, 2004; exhibition space: Bronx Museum of The Arts; artist: The 62; photography: The 62

59: Caleb Crye in Fire Suit, 2003; designers: Crye Associates; client: Lion Apparel; photography: Eric Fehlberg

61 top left: Fire Suit, prototype, 2003; designers: Crye Associates; client: Lion Apparel

61 top right: Fire Suit, final design, 2003; designers: Crye Associates; client: Lion Apparel

61 bottom: Fire Suit, sketches, 2003; designers: Crye Associates; client: Lion Apparel

63: Exoskeleton Skin, 2003; designers: Crye Associates; client: DARPA

65: Future Warrior, 2003; designers: Crye Associates; photography: Natick Soldier Center; client: U.S. Army

67 top left: *Silence: New Haven*, 2001, design for plaque; venue: Center Church, New Haven, CT; artists: Bradley McCallum and Jacqueline Tarry; designers: Matthew McGuinness and Francesca Jacchia

67 top right: *Silence: New Haven*, 2001, detail of exhibition prior to disturbance; venue: Center Church, New Haven; artists: Bradley McCallum and Jacqueline Tarry; designers: Matthew McGuinness and Francesca Jacchia

67 middle: *Silence: New Haven*, 2001, detail of exhibition post disturbance; venue: Center Church, New Haven; artists: Bradley McCallum and Jacqueline Tarry; designers: Matthew McGuinness and Francesca Jacchia

67 bottom left: *Silence: New Haven*, 2001, detail of
exhibition prior to disturbance; venue: Center Church,
New Haven; artists: Bradley McCallum and Jacqueline
Tarry; designers: Matthew McGuinness and Francesca Jacchia

67 bottom right: *Silence: New Haven*, 2001, detail of
exhibition post disturbance; venue: Center Church, New
Haven; artists: Bradley McCallum and Jacqueline Tarry;
designers: Matthew McGuinness and Francesca Jacchia

69 top: *Silence: Looking For...*, 2003, survey for grave
plots; venue: Neuberger Museum of Art, 2003 Sculpture
Biennial; artists: Bradley McCallum and Jacqueline
Tarry; designers: Matthew McGuinness and Francesca
Jacchia

69 bottom left: *Silence: Looking For...*, 2003, headstone/
plot location; venue: Neuberger Museum of Art, 2003
Sculpture Biennial; artists: Bradley McCallum and
Jacqueline Tarry; designer: Andrei Kallaur

69 bottom right: *Silence: Looking For...*, 2003, location
for gate; venue: Neuberger Museum of Art, 2003 Sculpture
Biennial; artists: Bradley McCallum and Jacqueline
Tarry; designer: Matthew McGuinness

71 left: *Silence: Looking For...*, 2003, gate; venue:
Neuberger Museum of Art, 2003 Sculpture Biennial;
artists: Bradley McCallum and Jacqueline Tarry;
designer: Matthew McGuinness

71 right: *Silence: Looking For...*, 2003, illustration for
gate; venue: Neuberger Museum of Art, 2003 Sculpture
Biennial; artists: Bradley McCallum and Jacqueline
Tarry; designer: Matthew McGuinness

73 top: razor wire, photo, 2004; designers; Crye Associates;
photography Eric Fehlberg; client: DARPA

73 bottom: Razor Wire Machine, final design, 2004; designers:
Crye Associates; client: DARPA

75: Razor Wire Machine, final design, 2004; designers: Crye
Associates; client: DARPA; photography: Scott Thompson

77 top and bottom right: Steps, final design, 2004;
designers: Crye Associates; client: DARPA; photography:
Eric Fehlberg

77 bottom left: Steps, concept sketch, 2004; designers: Crye
Associates; client: DARPA

79 top: *The Art of the Possible or How I Learned to Build
a Sled out of Trash*, 2005, concept sketch; venue: Exit
Art; artist: The 62

79 middle left: Sledding party, 2003; photography: The 62

79 middle right: *The Art of the Possible or How I learned
to Build a Sled out of Trash*, 2005, building process;
venue: Exit Art; artist: The 62; photography: The 62

79 bottom: *The Art of the Possible or How I Learned to Build
a Sled out of Trash*, 2005, exhibition detail; venue:
Exit Art; artist: The 62; photographer: Tod Seelie

81: sledding party, 2003; photography: The 62

83 top left: *The Art of the Possible or How I Learned
to Build a Sled out of Trash*, 2005; venue: Exit Art;
artist: The 62; photographer: Karen Sheasby

83 top right: *The Art of the Possible or How I Learned*

to Build a Sled out of Trash, 2005; venue: Exit Art; artist: The 62; photography: The 62

83 bottom: *The Art of the Possible or How I Learned to Build a Sled out of Trash*, 2005; venue: Exit Art; artist: The 62; photography: The 62

87: Future Force Warrior, early concept sketch, 2001; designer: Caleb Crye; client: U.S. Army

89: MultiCam™ and Future Force Warrior field testing, 2003; photographer: Pat Rogers

91: Truck on Canal Street, NYC, 2005; photographer: Matthew McGuinness

93: Convair 118, 1948; photographer: Johan Visschedijk, 1000aircraftphotos.com

95: Landfill, 1995; photographer unknown

97: Ducati 916; photography: Caleb Crye

99: Major Taylor, 1901, training in Paris;

101: Studio Exterior, 2005; photography: The 62

103: Matthew working on Dunhill at G2 Worldwide, 2004; photography: Andrei Kallaur

105: Hammer on the moon, 1969; photo: NASA

107: poster, G8, 2001, Italy; design: Matthew McGuinness and Morgan Sheasby

109: Lockheed SS71 Blackbird; photo: U.S. Air Force

111 top: *Nov York, Fuck Me/Read*, 1998; photography: Matthew McGuinnes

111 bottom: *Nov York: Act Up*, 1998; photography: Matthew McGuinness

113: Fractal Lettuce; photographer: Didier Le Botlan

115: Cyclone Roller Coaster, 2001; photographer: Alison Corrie

117: Critical Mass in Time Square; 2004; Photography: Andrei Kallaur

119: FedEx plane crash; photo: Department of Emergency Management

121: Flag on the Moon, 1969; photo: NASA

123: I Love You, Lamp Post, 25th and 11th St. NYC, 1 of 2, 2003; collaborator: Paul Sahre; artists: The 62

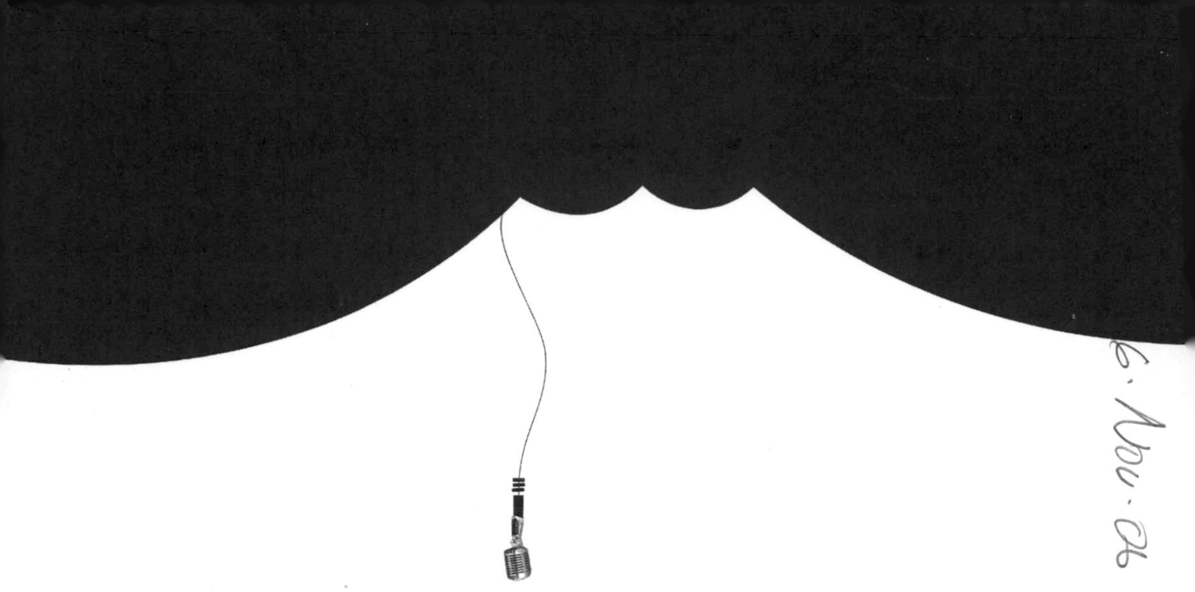